Creating Wealth &
Unlocking Value:

A Daily Affair

*-This book is dedicated to You and
to me*

Foreword

As of June 2018, the median American household had only $11,700 in savings, according to CNBC.[i] Even scarier is the fact that 29% of households have less than $1,000 in savings. In lock-step with this, one must look at the material awareness of people today. According to figures by the EPA, as cited by U.S. PIRG[ii], the national recycling rate hovers around 34.7%. That is despite the fact that 94% of Americans support the idea of recycling.

The typical urban dweller has likewise become so dependent upon the current model of consumerism, that the material handling efficiency of earlier generations of Americans, those who faced economic and social upheaval such as during the Great Depression and the World Wars, has been erased.

The aim of this book is to help identify the sources, strategies and methodologies to locate, create and multiply value in your day to day routines. We are surrounded by value, yet often do not see, or simply discriminate too much, and fail to grasp the inherent worth at your very fingertips.

As you will see, the ability to recognize value, and tap into its potential provides the best vehicle for replicating this technique "across the spectrum" to unfurl their combined synergies and release a larger yield. When you have unlocked these myriad micro-scale tiny steps forward and the gravity of synergy is working for you, you have created the ideal platform for force-multipliers to kick in and step up your yield potentials. The by-product of all this is a degree of financial security via savings and acquired wealth (unlocked value).

For those who are willing to provide passion to theses processes, this book is for you.

This book concentrates on easy to do steps to recognize inherent value and act on it. The three areas of focus are: Strategies for Value Creation, Material Repurposing, and lastly Product Substitution (application Beauty and Health).

This book represents my own personal experiences and is meant as an illustration of how I have generated my own value, wealth and savings.

8

Strategies to Unlocking Wealth

Value is in itself an integral component of all things material. An object's value can be relative, and fluctuates depending on particular need and relative demand.

Services also yield a value. In point of fact, any material that has been reworked or finished has a scaleable value higher than the pristine material itself. Examples: Gold > Jewellery, Flour > Bread, Wood > Furniture.

Money itself is a unit for value storage. It has little actual worth (unless crafted from precious metal), other than an agreed fixed storage unit of value. i.e. a 1 Dollar bill vs. a 100 Dollar bill.

Society today has developed to pursue consumerism. Endless buying of goods and services, many of which have short life-spans or usability cycles. This forces the participants in this system to constantly buy back products and services from the sellers.

In such a system, time itself becomes a commodity, which has been codified and traded relative to value storage units (money). As a result inefficiencies may and do occur. Material value may be discarded as a trade off to simply buy a newer or 'chic'er product or service. In doing so value is rejected in the form of the under utilized good.

This type of system is also very good at branding and convincing people that the state of their being will be enhanced by adopting the new good or service. A person can imagine a different lifestyle by buying into the glamour associated with the newer item or service.

This emotional usurpation causes waste and the loss of value. This is a double whammy as the buyer must shell out new cash to replace the older, while losing the value of the old in discarding. The formula involved essentially sucks wealth away at a faster rate and it becomes necessary to invest additional time, in the form of work hours, to adjust the losses as they accrue.

We will evaluate how to identify value and unleash it with scaleable methodologies to yield reclaimed value. Additionally we will evaluate and propose substitution methods, when possible to replaced a finished or branded product to tap into and reverse value outflows from your daily budgetary matters. Repurposing is also a highly effective tactic, which we will illustrate in this book. Let us begin!

14

Strategies for Value Creation

Source a method(s) for lowering the cost of every item you regularly purchase by 50%.

This is a widely sweeping method for retaining income, which is always limited and usually fixed.

The core idea here is to double spending power, while not actually spending the saved amount. This may mean switching brands, pausing purchases until sales can be had and so forth. This step is also a wide ranging one and shall require thought, analysis and bargain hunting. Examples of this in action may be the following: Establishing a bulk purchase ring of folks in your area that would go in on such group purchases. Say, for example you figure out the amount of meat you purchase to feed your family over the course of the month. Even if you are regularly buying meat only on sale etc., you need to do the math and figure how much you spend in this period. Once you have an idea of your base cost, you can proceed to calculate the price (50% below the amount) which you aim to undercut.

This is where the real work comes in. Sourcing the alternative. It may work out that you can find a farmer who will butcher a whole animal for a group of buyers. At this point you can use Social Media to organize a group of buyers to divide the meat amongst the group. Relatives may join in on the effort and reap the same savings. If your group falls short of buyers, you have alternatives to resolve this. If you increase your share of meat, you still have incurred no loss, per your monthly expenditure. This is where value may be applied. The excess meat you take on can be repurposed, refined or processed for resale.

If you turn the excess into sausages, beef jerky, steaks, cooked dishes, canned or preserved goods, etc you can unload those items at double their own value. This effectively means, not only did you half the price of the normal meat amount you buy per month, but by repurposing or increasing the second half, if you doubled its value by reworking it and selling forward, your original meat bill becomes 0 for the month. This is a win-win scenario, as you have created the value needed to half your cost or, in the case of the double purchase, effectively zeroed your cost.

The idea is to do this with as many items as is possible. This brings me to the next strategy.

Make a Cost Analysis for daily/weekly purchased items.

In order to establish a concept of value, this is a necessary and rewarding exercise in your research.
Let us use for an example for this analysis: tea. I shall use tea bags, as it is easier to quantify than bulk loose leaf tea and easier to grasp the value therein.

In my own usage and research, I have found the (so far) most inexpensive tea, which I buy at approximately 0.40 cents per box of 20 tea-bags. Thus, that yields 0.02 cents per bag. Cheap. It is not the normal black tea, but rather Fennel tea. This is healthy, lower in caffeine, carries health benefits, antioxidants, does not stain your teeth etc.

Now, if I reuse the bag a second time (should I choose to) I have cut the price to 0.01 cent per use. I have found for my personal taste that I can use the bag a second time and still reap the flavour. A little extra pressing with a teaspoon may coax out the needed flavour.

As we will see in the subsequent sections of this book, the value of the material has not been depleted. It is still possibly to apply the tea bag to other uses without discarding it at this point. Facial mask for under eye to reduce swelling and soothe the skin, or composting material for plants among many others. We shall return to this later under Repurposing and Product Substitution.

Thus, get a notebook or sit at your computer and compose a spreadsheet and crunch your cost analysis figures. Slowly you will fill in the entire gamut, most likely from the higher priced items downward. I would suggest you start in reverse, with the least expensive items and work your way up. Sometimes to key in on value it is necessary to see the smaller scale prior to the big and easy "low-hanging fruit."

Store Bought /Ready-Made vs. Home-Made Products

Another evident strategy is to run a cost analysis directed at ready-made goods vs. the cost for you to make them yourself. When you are thinking of those items that you routinely buy and are in high demand on your list. These items may be bread, canned soup, pre-made meals, deserts and so forth.
Obviously, by planning meals out in advance, you position yourself for savings. However, remember that, every time you buy a pre-made or ready-made solution from the shops and stores, you are paying for their

processing costs, labour and so forth. By baking your own bread, making your own pasta noodles, cooking large pots of soups, making home made deserts, you can unlock the value and lower expenditures.

I like to make a large pot of soup in the pressure cooker. The ingredients used are wholesome, fresh, healthy and unburdened by preservatives, salts, sugars, etc. and can last up to 3-4 days. That's a lot of meals (or complementary meal courses). Bread baked in the bread machine is a fraction of the normal loaf cost and more than double the amount of a single loaf as sold in the supermarket. This too (a single loaf) can last 3-4 days per person.

Now, replicate the cooking process on other frequent dishes. Gelatin is inexpensive as well. I buy fruit juice, which may only have a fruit content of 10%, and use it to make jello. Toss in banana slices or canned pineapple, or fruit cocktail and this is refreshing and very inexpensive. Gelatin is also quite good for bowel health. It is reputed to help with bowl function, contains collagen which is excellent for the skin and tissues, as well as digestion, blood sugar regulation, weight loss, bone strength, joint pain relief and better sleep.

Vary your deserts by making pudding, tartlets, cakes or whatever you find appropriate.

Other ready made ingredients can be made easily. A prime example is pasta sauce. If you like tomato sauce with your pasta, you can use, simply, tomato juice and cornstarch with a dash of salt and pepper and garlic for the ultimate substitution. Indeed, Spaghetti sauces can run relatively high, so this is prime real estate for unlocking value. Now, naturally if you can locate a supply of really low cost pasta sauce or even a free limited source, then naturally it goes without saying that you will opt for that. Your price threshold will already indicate the price point you are paying currently, so this is fully in your control. This moves us to the next point.

No (or as minimum as possible) Factory Made Meals or Components

For many this can be a sticking point, or point of contention. Speaking from the point of pre-made food items, these items maybe loaded with high salt or sugar content, palm oil or other similar low cost, uninspiring ingredients, which merely serve to build you up with visceral fat, exacerbate delicate health balances and similar. For me, I choose not to go this route if avoidable. I tend to stick to buying the fresh component items and construct my own meals with the quality of real items before heavy processing has occurred. Concerning certain cleaners or hygiene products, this may be unavoidable.

Dish soaps can be gotten relatively cheaply and are useful. If you use a dishwasher and use washing briquettes, this is hard to replace other than bulk based powders or fluids. I personally get the cheapest briquettes, which work admirably on my dishes. I also plan the wash cycle accordingly. Washing every 3rd day is possible if you make allowances. When I finally wash, I also break the tablets in half. Thus, I get double the washes (the 50% rule again here!).

The cost per wash (sparing electricity) is 0.03-0.04 cents only at this point, once again depending upon supermarket sales.

Super Sales, End of Shelf-life Products, Damaged or Mislabelled Goods Outlets

There are certainly times when you are able to find bargain deals. Once again, when you have established a complete cost analysis, it will be evident when you have hit the pay dirt you are looking for. You may be so bold as to carry your spreadsheet with costs on hand to compare, however, in this case you will no doubt be in safe territory to score high yields on the value spectrum. Now, it could be that you find items which you don't need, but using the previous methodology of upgrading/ unlocking value to scoop these up to realize their potential to your own network of friends, relatives, social media co-thinkers and so forth. At this point, the value become a small investment. Recall, that every time you raise the inherent value by repurposing or refining the goods, you will find yourself with surplus funds for your projects. These will come in handy later as great "leaves" or "sets," to set you up for force multipliers in your quest to increase the unlocked value yields.

I personally frequent a "damaged goods" outlet, where they have items which have either been poorly labelled (not up to snuff for some reason or another at full price). Sometimes there will have been a fire and the boxing may have a slight smoke odour or there could be other quality issues that prevent sale at the pristine shelf price. This place is filled with low cost food items, clothing, industrial goods, soaps and cleaners. A veritably large range of diverse products. Not everything can be sourced here, but, I know which items definitely can be. This brings up the next strategy.

Never Buy from only One Supplier

Diversify your supply chain. Shop around and know where to source what. Sometimes new items will arrive at the Damaged Goods Outlet. I like to become acquainted with the new items before I commit to buying them. Sometimes I will stroll into the markets just to see what the items are that have good value to me. YES! Value can and should be relative. What you need may be superfluous to someone else. Generally, basics and staple items have a rock bottom line, but off the beaten track and there can be bigger fluctuations.

By strolling around without intention to buy, I size up what is on offer and determine if there is value for me or not. But you should have multiple sources and locations to frequent. Keep your choices as broad as possible. I like to buy jars of salted pickles. It is possible to make my own, of course, and is inexpensive too. At this point I have not been able to replicate the best method for making them as I like them. I can find them in locations around town and I also know where I can find them at a rock bottom price. Actually, the difference is only 0.10 cents, however, I take this micro-savings. It is part and parcel of a system of micro-steps. It should add up to thousands of small decisions throughout my year, but I claim the value never the less. Perhaps because it is my passion to do so. It brings me all that much closer to where I want to be.

Thrift- Learn the Value Second Hand

Luckily, many people are already becoming familiar or have become accustomed to this tactic. In my own humble opinion, the type of items that show up in flea markets, Salvation Army stores, Red Cross and other second hand outlets have a lot to offer. To some people the concept of owning or buying something that has been used by someone else is offensive or repugnant. To my mind, the entire opposite should be true.

Evaluate the quality of things made these days for yourself. Large companies, for one reason or another seem more than happy to release flimsy plastic goods with an utterly short-lifespan. The durability of solid items once produced in slower paced times (1960s, 1970s, 1980s) seem to be resilient, whether it be wooden, glass, metal, fabric, even plastic! In many cases these items need a bit of cleaning, spiffing up, polishing or refurbishment of some nature.

I find these places excellent for acquiring furniture, artwork, glasswork and certain pieces of clothing. Books can generally be had in such places at very low cost.

Learn the Cleaning Value of Soda and Vinegar

Industrial cleaners can be costly and not work as well as one hopes. I am a big proponent in using soda or vinegar to clean grime or remove stains. As a fervent fountain pen collector, I fill my own pens with liquid ink and a hypodermic syringe. The operation can be a little messy and I often get ink on my figures. Soap or other cleaners can be totally useless to remove the dark green ink from my fingers. Surprisingly, soda and water work without effort. I scrub my fingers totally clean with a little soda and a bit of water to lather it up. After two goes I have immaculately clean digits! These common household components have so much information dedicated to them on the net about their particular application and uses, that I shall leave you to do the research wherever a need arises. Needless to say the cost savings is abundantly clear and these reagents are inherently safer then some chemical cocktails that are sold these days for cleaning.

Establish a Recipe-Trove which Adds Value to your Weekly Meals

Create a recipe trove of easy to replicate meals, which can satisfy your diet with the components you routinely acquire. You should have a diverse enough trove to cycle through and provide balanced nutrition, healthy choices, diversity, and foods you can process to scale. I like to make bread and soup for 3-4 days to supplement with my other meal components. Generally, I will have fresh salad as an integral portion of my meals. Since salad should be eaten fresh, I try to do no more than 2-3 days in a bowl at once, but this is entirely up to you. If I have sourced good cheap meat, in quantity, I generally divide into sub-parts. One is utilized for the meal I am preparing, then, I bag the other portions and place in the freezer for other meals in future.

My Recipe-Trove consists of different soups and stews, bread, crepes or bliny stacks can be eaten also over 2-3 days as a part of a meal with savoury stuffing, jams, honey or dairy based toppings.

I used to be a grand maker of Yorkshire pudding, which can be easily and quickly made and is good with savoury, home-made cornstarch based gravies. Another recipe that is quite easy and filling, oven baked olive bread (stuffed with nice whole green olives, garlic slivers, sesame seed and olive oil drizzle. A fling of parmesan is also quite nice here.

I recommend compiling a list of culinary easily made plates, which you can cycle routinely, should you wish to keep a semi-regular food schedule. This also provides extra sticking power to your fiscal discipline in maintaining the savings you need to retain your pocket money.

It is time to discuss the Home Budget, though, I suspect that you may already have this under wraps. If you do, perhaps you will determine something new herein, if not, kudos on your disciplined work!

Home Budget & Auto-Savings Determination

The whole idea for a Home Budget is to identify Variable Costs & Fixed Expenses vs. Available Income. Ideally, your budget will be realistic and accurate. If it is not. It is time to determine the problem areas and rectify (if possible). If the situation is tangled beyond this, then a strategy is in order to tame the runaway nature that is occurring.

Your thought to the budget should provide the grounds for a realistic level of Auto-Savings per month. This is cash which you, without thinking, can afford to set apart from spending. It should not be in the same pot of cash that you depend upon to deplete for your monthly expenses.

My minimum Auto-Savings Amount is:
$111 /€100 per month. Thus, $1332 /€1200 yearly.

This amount of cash is the <u>absolute minimum</u> I have saved in the period. Anything over this is my Surplus Savings (generally money from Value I have located and saved).

The idea for Auto-Savings is that it is rendered into an investment account. My goal is to keep this invested in growth for a 15-17 year period. I had some initial deposit on top of the base monthly, however, I am conservatively placing interest at 3% for the period. With this said and done, at the end of the period, the sum should be just shy of 30K, and this is at a percentage substantially lower than the promised percent parenthetically.

Any amount over the original minimum of the 111/100 figure that I choose to add into the mix will definitely provide an air of gravitas at the end of the investment! This is, to my mind, a perfect place to deposit a portion of value created from the below value strategies and efforts as a force multiplier. You should remember in your yearly tax statement to always report your ball park figure of miscellaneous income you've received over your normal salary. For this it is always best to check with your taxation specialist. I believe these rates (as far as my affairs are concerned) rank around 15.4% on profit, unless there are changes afoot. Ask your taxman to be sure, if you have sold goods or services that qualify. It may be that you end up owing nothing, but I would not leave this to chance. If your economising has rendered the savings, and you are not selling goods or services, then this may simplify matters.

Establish and Use a Barter Network, if None is Available

Bartering in the United States is a taxable endeavour; remember to check your responsibilities to be sure. If you have items that you have absolutely no need for, it could be that you may barter them. Locate people you have common truck with in these matters and determine what you have to offer and what is on offer. Some folks collect various items or scrap materials, which there may be interest in. Unless well established, this strategy may be hit and miss. Yet, it may just bring the Value you are seeking, filling a need or decluttering your unneeded material.

In more remote or smaller communities this is more likely to be feasible, due to the ease of relations with folks and the close knit nature of communities. I have often seen advertisements from people with old gaming consoles and loads of old games which they are interested in swapping or trading up, so there are options out there other than merely some food for a hair cut or what have you.

Trading up is a good, indeed, mutually beneficial arrangement, if your particular needs marry up properly.

Let's go back to Income briefly for my next strategy.

Extra Cash Flow/ Over Time Work/ Unexpected Income

If you have been given an opportunity to work over time, over your normal hours or you come into unexpected income, salary, instead of melting this money in pointless purchasing, consider dedicating a portion of this (at least) to a channel that provides a high turnover of the new Value you have unexpectedly received.

It could be additional Retirement Savings, other investment options, CDs or similar valuable transactions. Ideally, you set aside continuously for the moment when you have the required amount or if you are free to fluctuate the amount, then this is of no concern. Subdividing the amount is a good practice. If you have an extra 100. Hold 30 for sudden expenses, and dedicate 70 for the pot for your CD, Retirement, or what have you. If you are all good for pocket expenses, go ahead with the full 100. It is not a matter of you needing it in that case. The main import of this new money is it will act as a force multiplier on any investment you have planned.

Some people are leery of banks and prefer to hold on to cash reserves. Though there is risk associated with this, there is also risk with most matters in life, as a general rule. If you feel better about holding cash or even converting to gold and wish to store it at home, you should explore how much would be covered by your insurance, in the event of a misfortune. Also it is appropriate to have adequate storage for the treasure. A vault or safe (fire-proof) is always a good bet, if you hold high amounts.

Not spending this extra cash requires a high level of discipline. Indeed, a huge amount of Americans hold Credit Card Debt. According to recent statistics, the average U.S. household Credit Card Debt stood at $8,500[iii] as of October 2019.

The average number of credit cards per person is around 4 cards. These figures always make my skin crawl. It is difficult to understand living this high on credit. Anyone wishing to battle credit card debt, will want to seek advice on refinancing options and pay it down as rapidly as possible. Living on credit is the perfect fly-trap for bogging oneself down into working at the beck and call and behest of others. If one is so inclined to do so, that is a different matter. To me the process is so self defeating as to stifle one's ultimate max potential. So it seems logical to reduce the number of cards you use. How about 2 instead of 4?

Essentially, credit is a bet on the future. Since the future tends to be foggy, hedging your future freedom on credit is a weighted gamble. This brings me in line with the following strategy. Before we journey there, I would like to counter-say a possible question about the Retirement Savings or Investment you may be channelling to.

Some may same that with the investment you are also risking on a foggy future and gambling as well. If it is a matter of a Savings Account merely, or a Bank CD, these are FDIC insured, to be sure. Annuities are not FDIC insured.[iv] Some 401k plans have elements within them that are insured, however, generally they are not. Check with an investment expert to be certain in these matters, if the risk should nerve you.

Vacations and Cash Retention?

If you take a yearly holiday somewhere, one of the most costly outflows on the trip will be housing. This, of course, depends on what kind of holiday you like to take. For me, living in a cold climate, any warm destination is desirable. Living in Europe poses a variety of low airfare options to get to the holiday destinations relatively cheaply. In fact, within Europe it is not uncommon to cross borders, fly hundred of kilometres and disembark to the destination, for well under $111 / €100. Thus, the hotel, B&B or housing becomes the highest cost factor of the vacation.

Assuming the feasibility (it's always relative to each person), one method to pay oneself back would be to locate a property for purchase. If you do the math, Hotel rooms can run as high (easily) over $111 / €100 per night. Obviously there are cheaper options out there. AirBnB, for example, maybe half this amount, which is still not bad. However, the standard vacation time is 2-4 weeks in Europe. This quickly adds up, even at the cheaper rate. By purchasing I have equity in the property, which is the ultimate way of locking in the value of outflows from the present/past. Italy and Spain have so many inexpensive properties on offer, that it is not impossibly difficult to locate a bargain opportunity. So let's say I have vacationed routinely over 15-17 years here and my equity has been maintained (increasing each subsequent year). Remember, your work-life time is fixed. Once it goes, it gone. Purchasing is a premium way of retaining salary.

Upon retirement, it may be even feasible to retire to this property. During the years it may be possible to let this out on an AirBnB basis or other short term rental options. This, in turn, adds value to your equity! This is a way of ramping up the synergy in your potential value creation. If you have purchased the place outright with you own accrued cash, you are in premium position. If you have had to take a bank loan, your object would be to cancel the sum of loan and interest over the period you rent out. When you hit this mark, you have again effectively doubled your value. You are at this point getting the property for 0! You, at this point, have attained an optimum force multiplier!

Now, consider each and every big (or small) expenditure you face and how you can unlock the inherent force multiplier!

With the property option we have a sharp contrast to the credit card debt situation. There is no possibility for force multiplication under simple credit card debt. Whereas, with the property, you have unlockable value, which you can wield to harness the force multiplication, latent in its nature.

Remember, too, that any time you can rescue salary, it is a way of reclaiming value, which you have had to relinquish for one reason or another. By reclaiming it, you quash an inefficient utilization of your time spent labouring for it. You have also made it work for you, without having to do that work all over again. That may not even be possible, since time is fleeting in nature.

Urban Mining

What is Urban Mining? Apart from the industrial application[v], this, in my own parlance, is the taping a value in the place where you dwell. Whether you live in the wilderness, or an urban sprawl, you are surrounded by material of value. Identify it and claim it!

I live in an urban area, surrounded by thousands of co-dwellers, urbanites, etc. City-folk! City-folk are by their very nature wasteful consumers. Modern life seems to encourage wastefulness, laziness (or at least messiness) and sacrifices for time and vanity.

Case in point- people throw "trash" everywhere on their way to work or to school. Perhaps someone has moved and discarded "junk" etc. It is here where I am active. Let's start with the low hanging fruit first. Bottles, cans, and deposit value.

When I am moving about on my routines, I frequently spot discarded soda and alcohol cans and bottles. These I claim. In fact, if I have a short distance to cover, on some errand, I will frequently go on foot to cover the distance scouring for these items. My average net per week is approximately $4.47-$5.59 / €4.00-5.00. For the month this is about $17.88-$22.35 / €16.00-20.00. Now, let us assume that I have a few off months and on vacation I do not collect anything. The yearly amount of value coming in is in the area of $222/ € 200. If we still underestimate, to be conservative, the minimum achieved value, let us say that yields fluctuate and are under the projected amount. Even if the yields are significantly lower we'll like still have at least $167.60 /€150! That is $2514.00 / €2250 over 15 years time!

Imagine that you will have routinely offloaded your reclaimed value from this urban mining exercise into your retirement at 3%. We will see if multiply into $2770/€2450! Now think of how many months you will have had to work to attain the same amount of savings. It may easily be a half year's work, if not a full year! Even after claiming these amounts for taxation (should the amount qualify for reporting in your area) you still have a lion's share.

Unlocking this under utilized value should be a no-brainer for most. It merits only patience, vision and dedication to execution.

There are so many other examples of value in Urban Mining exercises in addition to this easy and clear option. Frequently people abandon furniture, solid wooden articles, other materials such as glass, cardboard, paper, metals, equipment, electronics, appliances, antiques or retro articles.

Fundamentally, you are only limited here by your creativity. When you see a value that you know how to unlock, then chase it. Other times, it may be necessary merely to hoard the material while you work out a solution or locate the need.

For this you should create your own spaces in the house where you can storage the material while realizing its value. When you have accumulated a sufficient stock of it you should effect your move. In your kitchen you should gear up for this by providing the receptacle, containers, jars, etc. for processing this material (food stuffs). We will return to this later in repurposing. Suffice it to say, even seeds, pits etc. from fruit and vegetables may serve for mining material.

Foraging is a long lost survival technique which has largely disappeared from daily life of modern city dwelling folk. I, myself, frequent the forest in search of natural items which I can purpose for value. Countless species of mushrooms can be located in the forest. (I only take mushrooms with a flat sponge side on the bottom, not the spoked ribs, since I know these much better and there is only one variety of spongiform underside mushroom which is poisonous, and it is red!). If you don't know your mushrooms, this can be a tall order. Berries too can be very high yield, but again, you must know your berries. I find blueberries (or bilberries), wild strawberries, raspberries, cranberries, rowan berries, rose hip, some fruit like apples, flower petals from the rose hip bush, leaves such as grape or oak, nettles, dandelion, clover, etc.

There are so many uses for these items: teas, jams, jellies, juices, soups, pies, cakes, freezing for winter or later usage. Such urban mining can yield in different ways, depending on how you realize them. I tend to collect deeper in the forest to avoid car pollution. I generally use these for my own home use, but one is certainty not limited. Preserves, pies, jams all make for charming gifts to family and friends. At any rate, you are limited only by your creativity. If I am unfamiliar with a produce or item, I will research it exhaustingly, first, to become acquainted with the safest methodology and considerations to be noted.

We shall discuss this topic more in greater detail under repurposing.

Portion Control

Let's go back to food, as this is prime real estate for unlocking value. By applying portion control, you can achieve a better ratio to your stocks and stretch to the best economy of use, having your supplies last longer. This should, ideally, be done by preparing a balanced meal with many components.

I generally consume small quantities of meats, and often plan for meatless dishes. My meal courses contain a full plate, however, they may be divided into a fresh salad portion, another vegetable dish, and a main course with or without a meat component. Bread and soup can be appended to a salad to balance out the nutrition and keep you full. By not overloading on a single dish you have variety and it is easier to adopt the portion control. If you like your spaghetti and meatballs as a whole dish, then take less and add some of your home-made bread to it.

When making meals I always make enough to serve and there is a leftover portion, which can be used for my work-lunch the next day. Food waste is minimal and infrequent. I have some fresh vegetables or fruits go bad, occasionally, mainly because I was producing so much value from other initiatives that the item became forgotten or I simply ran out of time. My bad. Still, this happens under 10 times per year. Closer to 5! Usually it is just a few pieces of fruit or veg.

Rubbery carrots can be the perfect soup filler, incidently. I don't throw these away, unless mouldy. I have chicken in the refrigerator, which I broiled three pieces. The pieces were big and I managed to eat only half a piece with my multi-portion meal, but I am afraid the chicken is getting long in the tooth. What do I do? These two are great in the pressure cooker with potato, a little broken spaghetti and a hand full of rice and spices as a chicken soup component. I merely remove from the bone and cube the meat. You can fry these prior with onion and carrot cubes and toss into the pot with the rest of the components, adding water and spices. Top off with some bay leaves and cook up. The pot of soup will last 3-4 days. This too is part of portion control. Any meat bones are excellent for your soup stock, so don't toss those before use!

Any piece of meat I have sourced I only use a portion in the meal I create. I always divide the entire piece and freeze the remainder. A 1 kg piece of meat can easily be subdivided for current meal and 1-2 freezer bag portions for upcoming meals, soups, etc.

This portion control is a powerful tool to use. Not only does it keep you healthy by preventing overeating, it also works as a force multiplier. You probably eat up to 3 times a day. Just under 100 meals a month (84). This is 924 meals in a year (minus vacation time of 1 month). So, the grand scale of this action is roughly equivalent to 1000 meals per year! Any value you can manifest in this process will render over time on the large scale, and can be equated in savings, less frequent shopping etc.

There are those who eat out frequently. So be it. Still, by practising the above technique, you may still recoup outflows and, in the end, will gain because this is a win/win application. I appreciate that restaurants can be a pleasure of life for many. If it is necessary, by all means, do it. However, recognize the nature of this, and try not to take it to excess.

Learn your Staples

Staples, those food items that act as anchors to your dishes, help to round out any meal. These may include such basics as:

Cabbage, Potato, Carrot, Rice, Noodle/Pasta, Flour, Buckwheat, Corn, Oat and the like.

These items are frequent repeaters as part of your overall diet and feeding plan. On these you should focus to bring the overall costs to the lowest possible denominator. Remember these items are frequent repurchases. Buying in bulk may or may not be an option for you. Definitely make a proper cost analysis of theses items and search for a plan or method to lower these items to that 50% (at least) level!

You may be able to do this through group purchase, or other mechanism. Just realize that as an item of constant repurchase (you always need them, so you return to buy) you have a lot of value to secure by keeping costs low here. Does that mean I may splurge on the other meal component items? Definitely not! This merely should be an open avenue of value reclamation due to the huge number of purchasing of these items over and over. An opportunity to realize the latent value of this essential constant repurchase.

Window-Ledge Growing

Growing herbs and small plants on your window sill is the perfect way to add value to your diet, food sources, etc. Seeds are inexpensive and often can be derived from the very items you buy from the store. Clearly not all seed are created equal (e.g. some hybrid seeds are sterile) not producing further fruit, but should you, for example, buy parsley or dill or other such herb from the store, these frequently can be bought already in potting soil. Put these in a larger pot or a long trough for continuance growth and continue to get the inherent value from them. Herbs can be somewhat pricey, so anytime you can grow these from seed, they represent a large percentage-wise value reclamation. A herb costing $1.11 €1.00 will be re-usable, if planted. A packet of seeds planted over and over, will yield many times their purchase value in savings. If you use these over the whole year, you have 50-100 opportunities to retain re-claimed value that price point! Large oaks from little acorns, isn't it?!

Learn the Value of Pickling, Canning, Preserving, Freezing and Drying

Making your food stuffs stay for the long haul is another hallmark of ancient societies. Today some use this, some don't. The largest value obtainable here is usually when it is the summer season and there are a lot of fresh produce on the market. Salad items will be at their lowest relative cost. Vegetables and fruits as well. This is clearly a good time to acquire as much as you can of these items and applying pickling, canning, preserving, freezing or drying. Also, there may be a sudden huge availability, sale or other such boon to acquire the items, free or at low cost. If you are already utilizing this method, brilliant. If not, learn more and step up your game! It is once again a method for enhancing your cupboard with foods of duration, flavour and bringing out that value.

Growing Produce of your Own

This naturally assumes you have a space and weather conditions for the opportunity to do so.

Figure out the amount of your budget which is affected by providing this. You may be able to displace a handsome proportion of purchases by doing so. If you are not able to affect such growing, try to figure out the way for displacing these costs. Is there some product or service that you can provide to off set these? This may go back to barter, trade and so forth.

Any time you have replaced an outflow with such a strategy, you will have more pocket money for your other projects, needs, investments and so forth. Examining a monthly food budget of $333.00 €300 and you can offset from this amount 111/100, then you will have reclaimed 33% of your already low costs. What can you do with the extra amount? Plenty. It may be that you have already lowered or eliminated the outflows, by other means. You should be able to see this in a comparison with your pre-action budget to your new value minded budget. What are you really spending on food after applying these methods? Have you reversed outflows altogether?

Renting vs. Owning

There is an old saying: "It takes money to make money." This may or may not be true. Your market situation will vary heavily on where you live. In my particular area (Europe) they have instituted a policy called "Right to Live." This provides owning the right to live in the particular dwelling. You still pay a form of rent, however, the funds needed to buy into this is approximately 15% of the value of the property. Thus, it is much more achievable money-wise to acquire. In comparison to renting, the square metre price is roughly 40% cheaper than renting from traditional landlords! For the price of a one room apartment, you can have a three room apartment! Very convenient.

Additionally, you have the right to sub-lease the location! Should you wish, you are positioned to rent a single room or the whole place. Putting a minimum $167.60 /€150 on top and renting it forward will unleash yet more value to you. In effect you can either find a cheaper flat to live in and rent out yours for the overhead, or should you be posed to retire, augment your retirement income with the excess! It may be that such an option is not open to you based on market factors or where you live. Research and find out how you can add value in your particular situation. It may even be possible to acquire a second property and pay forward to yourself via equity. Obviously, in such event, you will be saddling yourself with additional risk. The choice is ultimately yours and must be done with your own assessment and considerations. It is merely an avenue of opportunity for a value stream in your inflows.

Your Intellectual Industry

There are a myriad of approaches you may take to yield value from your time, talent, skills etc. Everyone has some kind of skill, interest, hobby, know-how and so forth. One interesting application could be via self-publishing. If you happen to be a blog writer and write blog articles, it may be that you can adjust or adapt these as chapters or segments in a book to be published. It is easily accessible in this form to the end user and will contain the work of many hours you have already poured into this. Making them into an e-book will help to spread your intellectual labours, ideas and can bring in ancillary inflows, in the form of royalties. There are many other intellectual applications to follow suit too. Think!

54

Material Repurposing

What is Material Repurposing?

Some people refer to Material Repurposing[vi] as "upcycling." Basically, it is the reclaiming of materials for reuse for other than the originally intended purpose. It can also be a form of recycling, such as multi-use.

I like to think of this in terms of the following terms. You have, in many case paid for something, yet there are additional uses for the item or material beyond its original first use. These items or material may also have been acquired at no cost. If so, this represents 100% extra value into your economy. Whatever you can generate from it will be pure value.

The thing about material repurposing, is this is usually the portion of the good that gets wholly discarded as trash. It falls into the waste product category of modern consumerism. From here you may pickup the best pearls in your quest for value generation. Let's look at some particular examples and techniques as to how and what.

Candle Wax

If you live in a place that is dark, or merely like to burn candles, you will often find yourself with the leftover unburned stubs. These are from candles both fat and skinny. I save these to remelt into new candles. You can make your own candles, use treated string (with non-flammable coating, or simply buy new wicks). The wax itself melts easily enough and can be poured into jars or forms and the wick suspended by a pencil or tooth pick in the centre.

Though this is inherently not a big monetary savings, think of it as follows: You have paid for 100% of the material when you bough the candles, yet the remnant (it may be as much as 10-15% of the candle) is difficult to use up. You must apply your brain to these issues and see the value of the wax, instead of simply trashing the remnant. This is an entire philosophy unto itself!

Meat Drippings / Grease from Cooking oil / Bacon Grease etc.

If you are buying hamburger, let's say 24% fat content, and you fry it up, the mass that melts away is a quarter of your purchase! You still paid the same amount per ounce/gram etc. So every time you repeat this you are throwing away that much of your money (a quarter of value). It's a significant percentage loss. How and why should you reclaim this?

Some people are irked by the idea of waste/loss etc. For them this is a no-brainer. If you wish to establish synergy in all your steps across all your outflows you will see the value. What applications can I find for this material I paid a quarter of the cost for? Well, for starters, why not save the pour off grease in a jar? When you have a full jar you can remelt and constitute with wax or paraffin as candles. You could also make soap with lye and the grease. I encourage you to be creative and find out a way that suits your own situation best. With a little scent and added components you may be looking at a home craft or additions to your own household needs.

Seed Reclamation

Seeds come out of virtually all fruits and vegetables you buy or acquire. Tomatoes, squash, pumpkin, dill and pickling dill, avocado stones, apples, oranges, lemons, pears, watermelon, cantaloup, corn, etc.

Anytime I have pumpkin, squash, cantaloup and such large items, when cleaning, I also remove and clean the seeds for roasting in the oven with salt and spices. These make a savoury snack and are a nice differentiation than simply eating popcorn, peanuts, and factory made potato and corn chips.

Health-wise seeds provide good roughage, fibre, and have there share of nutrients. All of this is good for the digestive system of most people. If you have no problem to eat these, this will make a nice little addition to your variety of snacks. This brings us to another repurposing opportunity.

Build Up A Seed Bank

As you come across seeds of different sorts, clean, dry and place into closed paper squares or envelops, whichever you have conveniently at hand. Not all seeds will grow, this is a matter of trial and error. Some hybrids will be naturally sterile. I have found that a huge amount of varieties will, nevertheless sprout. You can always test the seeds in question, first, if your idea is to trade up from your seed bank for other items, or barter.

Seed banks are also an excellent thing to have for the future. Ask any "prepper," who is convinced the end of the world is near. Having a large seed collection is a hedge against lean times. I certainly do not subscribe to the theory that the end scenario is currently likely, however, it goes without saying that you may very well be well served in the event of a deep recession or depression. It also costs you nothing to hoard and takes very little storage space. This is a survival strategy of olden days, and brings with it a possibly large value attached.

The Paper Chase

Leftover paper can have loads of different applications. This is abundant material and already currently heavily recycled. If you get newspapers, or come into them, by other means, you can use this for wrapping, drying, packaging, and similar uses. Depending on your use, you may be able to use it as a substitute good, as opposed to buying the ready made material. Scratch paper for drawing, writing, envelope and card making and so forth, can be very helpful in your value creation. If you heat with a wood burning stove or have a fireplace, you can burn as well as start the fire.

Cardboard, Glass, Wood, Plastic & Metal Material

Depending on your skills-set, you may be able to save and use items of these materials. Some communities have the opportunity to sell the recyclable materials at very basic amounts per weight or volume. Any recycling is good, and win/win. I personally keep a large supply of jars on hand for preserving, pickling, spice storage, other kernel or grain storage to increase life span and key the bugs at bay.

If you establish a small trading group, or in the process of your research, you may even find people who are specialized in a particular material, for example, wood scraps & lumber, metal, etc. If so, you could be on the look out to help them out, and receive some form of compensation, which is more suitable to your needs. This is in itself a great way to convert material from a static value-state, to bear its latent fruit. Everything coaxed out should be a 100% value yield.

Retro Items/ Unrestored Antiques/ Junk

Many things, once a quality item, become junked with age. For various reasons, flaws or spoilage. If your talents do not include restoration, you maybe able to find folks who do specialize in this. It is only up to you to scour the forums, clubs, and experts in order to unlock the value of such items. I have seen old meat and bread slicers, appliances, machines of diverse sorts, which were in their day quality pieces. If you have an item that can be given a new life by repolishing, cleaning, restored, the finished item's value, once back in a lovely condition, will be extremely valuable. In such cases, offer the tradesman the item for free to upgrade, with a nominal fee on the finished goods, should it be for sale (10-15%, for example). If you had a 100 year old bread slicer, which was in deplorable condition, only to be restored, it would soon attain its inherent new value. Claim your 10%! It could be tens to hundreds of dollars/euros! Not a bad win for you.

Source a Value for the Unneeded

If you have stuff you just don't know what to do with, you probably haven't thought hard enough. Old books, perhaps, baseball cards, magazines, model sculptures, art, whatever. Remember these are items to trade up, donate, barter and so forth. There are so many ways to unlock their value to you. Sometimes, merely by gifting someone with something that is in their area of interest, you will have made a very good impression. These gestures are often repaid in kind. At any rate, never underestimate the value of a donation or a gift. Knowing when to say when, as regards money is a powerful tool in anyone's arsenal too. Especially, when this is a zero-sum loss for you. It becomes a highly effect method for new future value!

Repurposing of raw or purchased materials

As previously mentioned, in the tea-bag analysis, tea-bags are quite useful. You may have the first use, re-use, then use the bag still as a beauty aid, under the eyes, or open the bag to use the tea-leaves in composting your plants. Egg shells can function as fertilizer, beauty masks, crushed into flour and used to cook, and a number of repurposing or recycling/upcycling ends.

Fat chunks from meat can help make a great soup stock, together with meat bones, or given to the pet dog as a tasty morsel. Beef bones can provide needed collagen, to aid in skin repair, etc.

Other food "leftovers" for repurposing maybe banana peals. These are good for polishing tarnished silver and many other uses. If you eat a bunch of bananas, look into their many fold uses. Its all about what suits you best.

Poultry feather are great for furniture and pillow stuffing, though, most folks aren't that close to the food production chain. Still, it warrants a mention.

I eat a lot of avocados and have a huge hoard of avocado pits. What repurposing is possible with these? The stones can be ground into a powder for tea, quite good with honey. Replanting, trading, selling are all options. There are a number of beauty options for their use on the skin.

Reused-Cork

Corks from champagne, sparkling wines and wines are a great item to reuse. These can find repurposing as drawer handles, cut up into disks and used under chair-legs and table-legs. Some people make art out of these, use them for bath mats, soak them in an alcohol-based solution and use them for candles to burn even. They can be covered in wax, for the same purpose. And while we are discussing re-purposing (this could have been mentioned in Urban Mining) pine cones from the forest can also be soaked in alcohol and burned as candles, or used to start fires in your fireplace or while camping.

Cork itself is a durable and flexible material for making a myriad of re-purpose items. They also make nice handles for small implements, fondue forks, etc. Wonderful as a material and very easy to work with.

Leaves

Leaves are ideal for repurposing. As briefly mentioned in Urban Mining, this material can be used in cooking, for example grape, maple or oak leaves to stuff with rice and meat. I once knew an Armenian lady who routinely gathered Maple leaves, since grape leaves were unavailable and stuffed these with meat, rice, carrot, olive oil and spices. Delicious "dolma!"[vii] You should likely take care to gather away from big roads where there may be car pollutants. At any rate, this was her own personal solution to suit her needs. I quite liked it.

Flowers & Leaves

Some flowers can, naturally be eaten in salads and so forth, yet, pressing forward on an addition repurposing, we can collect, press and dry forest or field flowers and leaves to make: bookmarks, art, collages and so forth. Some people buy and collect pressed plants and flowers. If you plan on pressing ferns, petunias and such for sale, check to see what interstate or international rules may be encountered. Some regulations may exist for selling bio materials, as such, transnationally. There is needless to say a huge arts and crafts opportunity, should one be so inclined.

Fabric Scraps' Functionality

Another ultimate material for repurposing is fabrics, cloth, string, yarn and so forth. These tend to be in abundance, and can often be sourced for free as an unwanted remnant. Fabric squares are great for quilting. The price of a blanket or quilt these days has gone through the roof. Many times fabrics can be sewed out of a number of strands and strips, by multiple runs through the sewing machine. These are the last word in efficiency. You can reclaim material out of the smallest fragment into new square units.

Larger oddly shaped bits are also sublime. I was once offered odd shapes of two different fabric remnants. The material, natural wool, was a downright shame to discard. The pieces fit almost perfectly together and nearly formed a ying-yang pattern once sewed together. Out of this I was able to craft a tasteful, if eccentric sleeveless vest with large pocket for a reading book or mobile phone. It was extremely satisfying, as projects go, and I added a unique article of clothing to my wardrobe.

Indeed, in general, I do not buy clothing. If I do acquire clothing, I can count on second-hand shops to round out my needs. Shoes and foot-ware are the most difficult items to source, but occasionally, I can locate these as well.

Pack-Rat Storage System

It is a good idea to set up places in your home, where you can pack rat your surplus materials. This is a necessary step, helping you to process your re-purposing goods. It should be well organized, by materials and easily accessible. The better you can storage this the easier in unlocking the value, and being able to visualize that amount, sort, and quantity of materials on hand, and keep them rolling for you.

I personally have a huge stock of cork, snail shells, avocado seeds, glass jars, among many others. At times you will have to do minor repairs to repair an object. As part of my Urban Mining, I frequently come into aluminium cans which have been crushed or plastic bottles missing labels. Kids will routinely damage these items ignorantly. I take as many as I think I can repair. With a crushed can, often a screw driver utensil will be needed to return the can back to an acceptable state for the can reader. It may be necessary to rip the thing open, straighten and tape back together, in order that it will roll properly. This provides for the original recycle intention that the distributor/factory has already paid for (and the end user too). They will be able to smelt the can, as it contains the same amount of aluminium and you will have helped save the Earth.

With plastic bottles the same holds true. So the idiot has taken off the refund label. If you find crushed bottles beyond salvage, the label can still function as a reader for the machine and the new bottle. Combine label with whole bottle, et voilà!Again you have returned the original value for the bottle's intended recycle.

Kitchen Repurposing Centre

As previously noted, it is highly desirable to establish a Kitchen Repurposing Centre. Set up so that you have the ability to clean, dry, process your metal cans, plastic bottles, composting agents, seeds, peels etc. The kitchen of today is not very well equipped for this. Apart from a trash can, and possibly a drying rack, you may need to put thought in how you wish to tool up for this value capture processing. Do you have storage jars filled with your salvage and supplies? Boxes, cartons, containers are essential and need to be systematic to work for you well.

Now that we have gone into detail as to repurposing, and some will say we have barely scratched the surface, it is important to grasp the big picture and unlock your own inner genie here. You are basically only limited by your creativity and how much time and effort you are prepared to give up to do these projects. Speaking for myself, I am happy to take this road, with the realization that it brings me closer to my ultimate goals and needs. Besides, it is not like there is anything on television to watch, in lieu of this pursuit. (Author bias, and proudly declared!).

Product Substitution

Habits and Product Substitution

Product Substitution is a primary method to divert outflows of your capital and create value. It builds the force multiplier latently situated in goods, which can be tricky to tease out. With practice, an eye to detail, and reflection on the possibilities, it is possible to grow your wealth and retain your hard earned cash.

Product substitution is extremely lucrative with items that are inherently expensive, due to the price of manufacture, advertising, delivery and transportation, insurance and so forth. Such items may include cleaners, beauty products, soaps, beverages, and the like, but they are not limited to these alone. Personal habits and practices can influence your need for a product to begin with. These fit in the category of substitution, but at the level of abstinence or self-control. In a word, discipline. Discipline is a key factor and function in the way of avoiding debt traps, high money outflows and similar results.

Let's begin to explore this all in depth!

Content/Service Substitution

What kind of content do you consume? What services are you using? I have adopted a very Spartan, minimalist approach in my consumption of content. Having removed myself from the TV cycle of uninteresting, time killing programs, I find life much more fruitful and enjoyable. I don't even have the time to watch television, serials, movies etc. Should I ever wish to watch something, I check its availability on free services such as YouTube and other net-based options.

Why should I pay for a service I have no time for?

I find myself satisfied by surfing access to blogs, YouTube free content, websites, free news websites and so on. I have applied this content substitution for all newspaper, magazine, video and audio services. It keeps my budget to the basic fees for connectivity, computer security, telephone access, electricity and insurance. It's a lean budget, which frees me up to cover housing, food and mass transit. Everything over this is pure savings.

Tea Spoon Pore Cleansing

If you ever have taken a hot shower, you will notice that your skin in soft and flexible. The pores are opened. The same is true after a relaxing steam bath or sauna. One technique I do is take a tea spoon to the skin and with a little pressure, I can evacuate the pores on my forehead, nose, cheeks and face. I am careful not to do it too hard, yet the amount of "butter" expunged is incredible! In so doing, I do not have to buy expensive facial cleaners to work the grease out. This is an example of product substitution based on habit. It is also very effect at keeping good skin for me. The spoon removes so much "butter" that it needs to be wiped clean after several such passes across my skin.

Coffee Ground Facial Scrub

Re-use your coffee grounds as a facial scrub. This is a perfect product substitute. Beauty products, many of which are over-rated in my humble opinion, are pricey and the end result can be had via a different agency. So why pay through the nose (pardon the pun) for your facial scrub?!

Citrus Peels/Rinds

Citrus peels, such as orange and lemon, can also be utilized as a facial scrub, infused in oil and used to whiten the skin, dried and used as bath scents and the list goes on. They seem to function fairly well as insect repellents in potted plants to ward off the flying pests, in addition to the above uses.

Avocado Pits

Avocado pits can be used as a facial scrub as well as in a home-made shampoo with normal shampoo or Dawn dish-soap.[viii] There are, naturally, many different recipes for this and many other applications too. The point here is to instil a sense of product substitution per se.

Tea-Bags (again)

Tea bags are sublime for soothing bug bites, face mask, under the eyes to rid yourself of dark circles, applied to rashes for relief, provide relief for sunburn (that requires a lot of tea-bags!), diaper rash relief, etc.

Dried tea bags can also be premium fire-starters in the wilderness. If you carry a tin of alcohol pre-soaked tea-bags or wax covered ones, these will do the trick!

Another interesting application of tea-bags in action, as a dying agent! I wish I could take the credit for this, however, this was the brain child of a Ukrainian friend. I had woven squares of some fibrous nature weave. There were four 1-metre squares and I needed to make them into one long mat for my kitchen. My friend took some light coloured yarn, which was at hand and died them in the tea bag water, which darkened the yarn to the precise colour of the woven squares! It was the perfect sourcing and substitution for the store made equivalent from the hardware store. Impressive application and all had for 0 cost.

Egg Shells

Egg shells can be crushed, as previously noted, for facial masks. These help to lighten and white the skin. Once again, a prime candidate for product substitution. Some people even consume egg shells for added calcium and other minerals. These should be properly washed, for anyone with such a use in mind.

Cucumber skins or cucumber slices

Many beauty mavens have already been practising this application to hydrate under the eyes. It is a practical and wide-spread product substitution in usage. These reduce redness and swelling of the skin, and nourish acne-prone skin types.

Banana Skins (once again)

Once again, apart from silver polishing, banana skins can function as an under the eye application for the same reasons as cucumber, and reputedly whiten teeth, even.

Vinegar and Sea Salt Foot Scrub

Vinegar/ Apple Cider vinegar and sea salt is a great product substitution as a scrub for callused and stinky feet. Vinegar/Apple Cider vinegar and Epsom salt are also a great soak for feet to clean. Epsom salt removes moisture from your feet making it harder for bacteria to thrive inside. Remember to check how much water you need to mix into the soak so as not to go too acidic! Apple Cider vinegar is more alkaline than normal vinegar, which is slightly acidic.

Honey and Sugar Body Scrub

Honey and sugar are suitable as a body scrub to help exfoliate your skin and tighten skin. There are a wide variety of recipes available. Find the recipe which is best suited to your skin. This is not only a great beauty and skin care tip, but price-wise more feasible a solution for skin care than the pricier commercial options, in my own experience.

Other Excellent Body Scrubs

Green tea, honey, ginger, and coffee is another scrub which you can easily try out. Remember that exfoliation is a good way to promote collagen production for smoother, even skin. My experience is that 1-2 times per week is adequate to my needs and my skin is not overtly sensitive.

If you have skin issues, do your research properly and in advance!

Home-Made Underarm

You can craft your own underarm with as little as Coconut oil, essential oils, baking soda and corn starch. If you are not afraid to experiment, or can find the best recipe which suits your needs, then this is another area of stemming cash outflow and product substitution. It should be geared based on your usage. If you do not use so much, it may not be an issue or interest of yours.

Apple Cider Hair & Baking Soda Wash

For exfoliating sebum in your hair, an Apple Cider and baking soda based paste is an option.[ix] This is a very exciting product substitution in itself. To the extent you totally remove/substitute shampoo using this method, you have a large scale savings over the months and years you will apply this! Do the math, if this is an interesting option, and figure cost savings based on month, year and multiple year applications. You may have more free cash than you originally surmised you could rescue by this particular substitution. This all depends on how frequently you wash. This brings us to my next substitution/habit.

Hygiene and Thrift

In my own experience. I just cannot wash my hair every single day. It could be my own age and diet. I just don't know. I wash my hair every third day. This is because daily washing is so destructive to my hair, it overly dries it out. So by alternating with a spare wash-free day in between, my hair retains enough "grease" for softer hair overall. I generally do not use conditioners, so this option works best personally for me. Of course, if I need to cleanse or wash my body, due to heavy perspiration, I do wash with soap, but skip the shampoo.

By cycling my showering, I also reduce water consumption, needless to say, and keep a degree of thrift and hygiene which is suitable to my needs, without overdoing it either way. (Too much/too little.)

The Pumice Stone

A pumice stone is mandatory by my own needs, to remove calluses and keep the feet healthy and soft. With vinegar and dish soap and the pumice stone will come clean after its multiple uses. A stone will not function very well if it gets loaded with your old skin, so keep it in good working order by cleaning it out with a scrub brush, dish soap, and vinegar. The stone will last much longer too. Its all about caring for your hygiene, while being frugal.

Life Style Choices/ Regular Exercise

Regular exercise will keep you fit, stabilize your health and provide essential cardiovascular health for a decent stamina and good resistance/ immunity. Walks, jogs, skating, blading, swimming, stretching, HIIT; whatever, you can manage routinely to keep your body in efficient shape and health. I put this habit under product substitution, as I consider it a pre-emptive or pro-active choice/habit which will deliver you from possibly unnecessary future expenditures.

Eating the Balanced Diet

By eating the balanced diet, across the entire food pyramid, you set yourself up for healthy choices. When you are healthy and active, it propels you farther and faster. Remember the importance, as previously discussed, of portion control! Limit highly destructive and addictive habits/substances such as alcohol over-consumption, tobacco use, even vaping has been the focus of many health studies as a possibly harmful pursuit.[x]

Fasting Routines

Fasting may not be for everyone. I can only address how it has helped me. I use routine fasting regularly, though my version may be entirely different than it is for others. In my case, I will usually not totally avoid food (though on some occasions I do exactly that!), while observing that I am consuming enough water to stay adequately hydrated. When I fast, I may merely eat a small portion of plain rice or oats with butter or milk once during the day. The rest of the day is all water. No tea or coffee. I manage this type of fasting at least once every ten days or three times per month. It is born out of discipline. To achieve an internal cleansing, to stay thin, to get the boost it gives when I come back off it. There is a boost of energy associated with this for me and a clarity of mind, which I receive from it. It is also a time of reflection. This brings me to the next habit/ substitution.

Meditation and Prayer

Meditation and prayer is a vital (for myself) part of my thrift vision and it provides me with the energy and the reflection to accomplish my goals. With all the focus on material costs, the bottom line, and money, it is essential that one is rooted in one's faith. It is prerequisite to evolve the spiritual dimension of one's being and devolve the materialism of one's life to succeed. This is the effective counterbalance to avoid becoming obsessed with merely crude material and money motives. It is seeing materials as part of a natural order, which is located in its own specific place. They provide a means for self-fulfilment, but not the ends! Respecting this is an important aspect in keeping priorities and a balanced morality. By recycle, upcycle, barter, product substitution one is essentially paying great respect to the universe around and the ecology of the World. So pay it forward and continue to conserve.

Optimism

By being optimistic, this habit on its own, is a powerful asset to have in your skills set. Yes, optimism is as much of a skill as any. Some people will never have this. They have not had the reflection or seen the grandness and nobility of the endeavour.

Radiance through positive directed thoughts, emotions and attitude will position you for success and, as such, should be regarded as the ultimate methodology or technique in the battle for value recognition and creation.

An individual who is negative, destructive, antagonistic, impatient and bitter will enjoy less success than an optimist. The optimist is a beneficial opportunist who knows how to craft win/win scenarios and as such enjoys trust.

<u>Summary</u>

Virtually anyone can practice the techniques of Value Identification and Creation, Urban Mining, Material Repurposing, and Product Substitution. In fact, none of this is new. People have used them all, to a certain degree, since the dawn of time. The key is to maintain discipline, passion, and optimism in their practice.

Let's recap some of the saved or rescued value we have managed to unlock by employing these methods.

Lowering cost on everything you buy by 50%

Let's assume that your food and consumables budget is $444 / €400 per month.

Achieving this will unlock $222 / €200 per month $2442 /€2200 for 11 months (assumes a month of vacation away from home.

If you rework, resell, or improve anything and up-sell, you can also increase your margins or get your cost to the 50% (if not better), such as the meat example we discussed.

Auto-Saving a Minimum Amount ($111 / €100 for Deposit/Investment Plan

This will yield you $1332 /€1200 yearly, of non-spent funds.

Vacation Rental Reverse /Equity Retention

This will be variable, however, the base rate of $55.50 / €50 per day for two weeks e.g. 14 days is ($777 /€700). If longer, apply figures at scale.

Sub-rental of the Right to Own variety Lease

Assumes you move to another lower rental at the same cost as your current (though you may be able to better the rent price to your advantage)-your conservatively estimated profit is $222.00 /€200 per month (on top your cost), or $2664 /€2400 per (12 month/ year).

Portion Control, Self growing of some food stuffs, Urban Mining (edibles), Urban Mining (recycling), barter, trade, balancing meals, keeping fit, Product Substitution, Good Habits

These all combined can be highly variable and depend on your long term success in implementing solutions.

Even if we only limit ourselves to the Urban Mining (recycling), of deposits on bottles and cans, the yield that I enjoy is on the order of (very conservatively stated) $167.60 /€150! obviously, the true goldmine can be had here if one gets serious with other efforts over just cans/bottles!

I do believe that much more can be achieved by this grouping, yet I am willing to play devil's advocate to make the point.

Without taking into consideration extra money you have in your salary that you save over your monthly costs and without considering any over time, extra revenues, etc. let's proceed to tally the low ballpark estimation of our efforts:

$2442 /€2200
$1332 /€1200
$777 /€700 (equity savings rescued)
$2664 /€2400
$167.60 /€150

TOTAL $7382.60 /€6650

I have included the equity savings rescued back into your pocket, as it represents wealth returned or retained at your disposal. Obviously your actual equity is greater, based on the payments you contribute monthly, but I wanted to highlight wealth you held, due to foresight and diligence.

Any salary left unspent is unaccounted here, as any funds generated from your unlocked value/ created value. Of course, taxes will come out of these figures, however, by figuring at such a conservative level, you can see how these figures will easily maintain themselves.

In actuality, if you get serious with your endeavours, one can see it easily possible to go well above the figures above.

Should you be compounding the reclaimed value you will also substantially grow this over time.

The figure of $7382.60 /€6650 over 15 years, without compounded interest is a massively stunning: $110739 /€99750

Compounding at 3% for the same period is rounded approximately: $138000 /€135000.

This is not your left-over salary or any overtime, but the low-ball figures we applied. Certainly an appealing amount. If you are a low earner, around 30K per Annum, you will have recovered 4.5 years of salary over the period! That is 1/3 of the Savings Period of 15 years!

It is hard to imagine a more efficient method. Anyone can affect this result and you don't have to rest to hair-brained Marketing schemes or Drop Shipping wonders. Just be patient and prudent! It is my wish that you reap some form of benefit or improvement by having read this and touch on the basic wisdom of the approach.

I hope you may employ and, indeed, improve on this model, getting the most out of it.

Good luck and many blessings!

MD Montandon

December 29th, 2019

Footnotes:

i   https://www.cnbc.com/2018/09/27/heres-how-much-money-americans-have-in-savings-at-every-income-level.html

ii https://uspirg.org/news/usp/it%E2%80%99s-%E2%80%9Camerica-recycles-day%E2%80%9D-united-states-set-recycling-success

iii https://www.thebalance.com/average-credit-card-debt-u-s-statistics-3305919

iv https://www.immediateannuities.com/state-guaranty-associations/

v   https://en.wikipedia.org/wiki/Urban_mining

vi https://www.investopedia.com/terms/r/repurposing.asp

vii https://www.allrecipes.com/recipe/25310/dolmas-stuffed-grape-leaves/

viii https://www.onegreenplanet.org/lifestyle/how-to-make-shampoo-out-of-avocado-seeds/

ix https://www.treehugger.com/organic-beauty/no-shampoo-experiment-six-months-later.html

x   https://www.fda.gov/news-events/public-health-focus/lung-illnesses-associated-use-vaping-products

.

www.ingramcontent.com/pod-product-compliance
Lightning Source LLC
Chambersburg PA
CBHW021452210526
45463CB00002B/749